AfterKill

Poem Story

From

Timothy Brannan

Front Cover Art: Original painting by Timothy Brannan
Back Cover Photo: Lana Brannan

Other Works

Ho'okele the Navigator
Shards of the Urn
THE END
TEARS OF ALLAH
TEACH
Manhattan Spiritual
Into the Elephant Grass
Adventures in Another Paradise
'74: A Basketball Story

© Timothy Brannan 2015
ISBN 978-0-9861646-0-6

Published by Gemini Publishing LLC in the United States of
America June 17, 2015

To my wife Lana

Table of Contents

I

There's Weather out to Sea

Obviously

There's weather out to sea

And it'll soon be coming ashore

The clouds will bring rain

And more of the same

When we are expecting more

It'll bring with it wind

And lightning and thunder

In clouds of deception galore

It'll bring with it pain

It'll bring with it plunder

It'll bring with it peace and war

While she's tending the garden

Of fruits and delights

While she's tending the garden

Of sounds and lights

While she's tending the garden

Of light and of love

The storm still rages above

The great ideas of women and men

Are finally just sawdust on the floor

That's wept over and swept up

And used to stuff

The straw men at the door

Oh, obviously

There's weather out to sea

And it'll soon be coming ashore

It'll bring with it wind

And lightning and thunder

In clouds of deception galore

It'll bring with it pain

It'll bring with it plunder

It'll bring with it peace and war

Yes, the clouds will bring rain

And more of the same

When we are hoping for more

The Osprey

After the hour strikes

The osprey sinks its claws

Into a larger than usual catch

Under the macro lens and laws

Of birth and life and death

And the occasional pause

Flash of sun bolts sling

Wing to wing

As osprey soars ward sky

Like rogue SAM

Into sunrise spring

Talons excoriate the pi

Still struggling to be more

Than merely food for thought

Or muscle against the oar

While he contemplates

The conundrum the weighty fish has wrought:

"I am therefore I kill to eat."

"I kill to eat therefore I am caught."

Attention to Detail

In attention to detail

Great lies are grounded

It's in attention to particulars

Truth may be well-founded

It's in the minutiae

That truth and lies

Lay simultaneously

Side by side

And face to face

Before our eyes

Gator and Merlot

Later after the gator and merlot

He resolved the conjunctions in his eyes

Before he ripped

The participles from her lips

And the gerunds from her thighs

Where resides the roe

Of the gator and merlot

Hacked Hai Ku & Tanka Twisted

The NASDAQ crashes

The Dow goes through the floor

Waves of ashes

On a digital shore

See old Dick dying

See aging Jane crying

See ageless Spot still relying

Such lack of freedom will just provoke

Another hurricane spawning

Amidst all that ardor

Before the dawn

Wear the woven

Spare the cloven

Take alms for complying

With destiny drawn

Freedom is no yolk

In a red hot pan

Over a white hot fire

No grand harness

Of temptation

And unbridled desire

Freedom is no joke

Encased like fiber optics

In a sheath of wire

Freedom is just a stick

In the mud

That cannot hold it

I drown in the sound

I am so confused

By the voice I hear

When I open my mouth

When I adjust my ear

That I often feel unscrewed

Or headed for a drought

For, you see, my dear,

I actually drown

In the sound

Of what I hear

When out and about

From the unspoken and the said

About gold transmogrifying into lead

To the necessity of being fed

Yet I have lost my way in the maze

Of well-reasoned highways

Each path blinded with

Frenzied blades of glass

And our progeny

Born on bended knee

Amidst the morass

And the inevitability at last

Of becoming dead

Or being recast

The ruse and the muse

I do not know

What is the ruse

I only know

I have no use

For aggravation by

The news

Or inspirations of

The muse

Poet and Poetry

What can the difference be

Between a man who is a poet

And a man who writes poetry?

I've never been able

I've never been able to write

The poem I wanted to

About the incessant life fight

As it obtains to me and you

I always thought that dying

Would involve some kind of trying

And would not ignite

The delicate fuse between us

Despite all the love and fright

And the penance that was due

Now I know that I was just time buying

For a more resilient glue

Way

A note I cannot play

A word you cannot say

A carcass we cannot fillet

Or flay

Is that we what say

Lies yond ever the for be reach

Of each

Us of today?

All for . . . .

All for the freedom of what is wild

All for the life of one small child

All for the lover that waits by the well

All for the devil that sends us to hell . . . .

Gurgles

As long as those who

Remember them live

Those who died young

Lived best

And those of us left

Holding the bag

Are doomed to

Never forget

The pain in our chest

When that final request

Gurgles past our own ruptured lips

Sanity's cloak

A spot spreads across the page

"And I dwell in the house

Of the lord forever"

Rips from the lips of a sage

In fear that the single dark spot

Will finally out blot

 Gladness

As well as wildfires of madness

With words of worship and of rage

Cowering in the cloak of sanity

Madness becomes lucidity

For this or any age

Pretense Abandoned

I have abandoned the pretense

Of everything

Except

The precept

Of abandoning

The pretense

Celestial hook slide

Trying to avoid

The glove of god

With a hook slide

On a very close play

The throw awry went

On the side of the bag in

The shortstop gang agley

II

Right the ship!
It's taking on water
To starboard
And soon to port
It will founder

All hands on deck

To foil the wreck

All hands secure

The spider webbed mirror

What holds the cure for

Sideways and down back

Amidst the swell

Of panicked furor

Lamentations (of the) Past

Wail, wail, the lamentations (of the) past

Long enough to make matter no longer last

Where the rip currents rip with no deterrents

Precisely aligned between guilt & grief

And tenderly balanced knowledge & belief

Their rants and rent clothing feeding flames so hot that

Hell would melt like a polar ice cap

Cradled in the god of desperation lap

Wail, wail, the lamentations (of the) mast

Never again will demented depraved deprivation

Be permitted to substitute for actual verisimilitudization

No one please, one only appease the situation

That is the tease built in of the pulse itself

Itself a tease for something else

So, ok, ok, ok

Wail god damn it anyway

Wail away

Self-imposed lunatic that you are

Sit

Stay

Wail as you wailed never again before

Awaiting hungry the wolf ajar door

In the beginning

To begin with

We begin with and from

The wrong first rung with

We always on come

That irrefutable part with

So we say

That there is a plan from the start with

There is some tion explana

forthwith

For the reindeer and the sleigh

There is certain savvy with

The hardening of the heart

And the winning of the day with

I

The rot begins

With the dogged relentless ruse

That somehow we were spit

Upon this speck of grit

To be of some fucking use

That somehow it might matter

Whether we act or we chatter

Or whether we decide

What our eyes will see

Or will something else guide

And decide for we

There will always be

That prayer or chant or plea

Claiming we are not the whore

Of space time or before

For we are imbued with purpose of a sense

After all

And that informs our every ascent

And each subsequent fall

II

Just for this moment

Can you sense the foment

Of all that is necessary

For you to fight or flee

And what the consequences might be

If there is actually

No purpose to inform thee

Or thine own philosophy

III

Wail, wail on

Sail, sail sun

Undone! Undone! Undone!

Delve none unsung

Yet we *are* delved and undone

And unsung for the price of just one

Your daughter or your son

Your only worship or your exclusive fun

Facing down the starter's gun

In the only race you have ever run

IV

Disparaging or despairing

The reddest herring

Still produces offspring

For which there is no accounting

Except by blaming a sense of purpose

That will, not so gradually, usurp us

Absorbing the anguish of absurdness

That lingers each forever in of us

Into the meaning sponge of fulness

There we become mingled and mangled

In the star-spangled tangle

Of space time rust

And of every cogent angle

Of hate, love and lust

And the actions all of us

Take

We

Must

listen

Listen closely and you can hear

My tears plopping in the puddled mud

Beginning their path toward

Hydrogen & oxygen

Then once more to muddled pud

Again

I am responsible for the deaths of so many

From the shallot to the kohlrabi

From the rattlesnake on the lone prairie

To buffalo for as far as you can see

And for, most regrettably,

My friend as well as my enemy

In the midst of where nothing is everything

How far do we have to go

How far do we have to come

How far must we travel to glow

In the blizzards of the sun

Slipping through my fingers

Slipping through my fingers

Life rips at my heart

Sliding through my fingers

I couldn't grasp it from the start

As it kept me at bay

With death of a million cuts

And a really fast getaway

The skill of which my father was most proud

My father's greatest skill

Was his ability and will

To exact more slices from

A tomato or an onion

Than just about anyone

Including his only son.

No heart at the heart of it all

There is no heart

At the heart of it all

There is only a fart

In a crumbling mall

A strangled shout

In a darkening hall

Begging that you not

Kill it at all

(It kill all you at

But stand up to it

And)

In a shrinking voice

That sounds so small

(Surely not by choice)

But the voice of a doll

Chanting its mantra

At your beck and call

And continuing to rout

The bludgeoning doubt

That the heart of it all

Is to lunch out

The froth

The froth swellfell over shattered sea shells

And buried the crabs once again

The froth foamed across their sandy dwells

As the sailors shoved and steered their craft in-

To the froth and foam of honor and of sin

I and I alone

Can deprave you!

Screamed the captain's voice

Without so much as an inflection

Betraying that he had any other choice

I and I alone

Can enslave you!

He bellowed above the fray

Of froth and foam and sodium chloride spray

It is my craft that makes you whole

It is my craft that spirits your soul

It is my craft that keeps you cold

Safe from the bacteria and the mold

That settle in when you grow old

I and I alone

Can save

You!

He gurgled beneath the last next NaCl wave

III

Give you what I can

You ask me for some pity

And I could give you none

You ask me for a daughter

And I will give you a son

You don't understand the nighttime

You don't understand the sun

I only give you what you ask for

When there's nowhere left to run

I don't want to give you anything

That will cause you pain

I don't want to give you anything

That will make you complain

I only want to give you

What I can

Out of the darkness sprang the light

From the depths

Of the darkness

Came the light

Obscuring the source

Of the blight

He straddled

The middle

Between sightless and sight

Hoping he could somehow

Still survive this life

When out of the darkness

Again sprang the light

Back into the darkness

Like an Osprey in flight

Was it the presence

Or did it just show the way

Did darkness obscure the set

Or did it make the play

Everything is still until it moves

Everything is still until it moves

Everything moves when comes its hour

Everything remains still until it moves

With appro speed and priate power

Everything moves with velocity and force

Everything contributes to the meteor shower

Everything is still until there's no recourse

Then moves inexorably toward its tower

Why wouldn't my father teach me how to draw

It's so sad to say

But we did alight

In a godless way

On a less god night

In a godless play

About a less god plight

I still can't recall

Why it matters my way

But I needed an answer to stall

The question today

Why wouldn't my father

How to draw me teach

Incredible

Incredible

That would be

So incredible

From sea to sea shine

You & me to dine

Incredible

Incredible

As it would seem

You in first a dream

To me came

Incredible

Incredible

Thoughts long a

The way

To ing us be

To having our say

Incredible

Incredible

Now it's

Up for the count

It is

Clean out that account

Incredible

Incredible

Now it's

In penny for a

In pound a for

Now it's

Money for go the

And not ing found be

There's a time

There's a time you go

There's a time you stop

There's a time you open

And there's a time you lock

There's a time for a microscope

A telescope

Or a clock

A time to elope

Or take stock

And a time to solve a puzzle

With razor cam's Oc

I can right a wrong

I can right a wrong

I can wrong a right

I can write a song

I can pick a fight

But I can't seem to find

A pathway back to you

I can't seem to divine

A way to construe

How I can be so strong

But still can't seem to mine

A clue as to what went wrong

With all those ties that bind

Defined and Identified

Lines define

The space that serves

As closet for my thoughts

Designed for wine

And hors d'oeuvres

As well as other shoulds and oughts

Space identifies

Where the lines fell

With sufficient clout

To hang ideas on as well

As keep the maggots out

Too far gone

Too far gone was his deliverance

Too far gone was where he'd die

Too far gone to make a difference

Too far gone to heave a sigh

Too far gone to be an inference

Too far gone to continue the lie

Too far gone for those who loved him

So far gone he'd become his antonym

Too far gone like distant chatter

Too far gone for us to see

Too far gone for it to matter

Too far gone for you and me

Too far gone to surrender anything

Far too gone to even ping

The implausible vacuum

In that place where

You live beyond

The pistol and the magic wand

Dozens of volcanoes

Lurk beneath your floor

Waiting to erupt as

They have before

But life is coming up roses

Before they've bled

It's coming up crude

Under your bed

In an exhibition of poses

By the quick and the dead

Displaying attitude

Instead

fragments of his deconstruction

I

He knew there were ideas that spoke to all

No matter how large or infinitesimal

But he could compulsively recall

Only the places he had not been at all

It was mong those a

Non-memory memories

Where lies came truth be

And truth volved into lies de

There experienced youth he

And all its alibis

From most feared of all fears

To most lulled of all lullabies

In one great blast of feast or fast

He finally felt

In a single flash of fire and ash

What he'd been dealt

In one great feast of fast or blast

There he knelt

To make final his cast

In a single flash of fire and ash

II

Isn't it strange

How much people change

When they haven't really

Changed at all

Where is the good guy

When you need him

Where is that girl

With the golden heart

I don't know why

But I really miss them,

Since the world has

Rended them apart

III

Around the bended

There's foe or there's friended

That's all we

See ever will

The in ended

Just the end there

In the end where

That's all will

Ever be

Reality

Squeaky new leather

With a murmur murmur roar roar

From the throat

Of the crowd

From the heart

In the shroud

Behind the lock lock

On the door door

Sea cotton dress

How ugly she looked

All cinched up and cooked

Like basted turkey nonetheless

How ugly she looked

All cinched and hooked

In her celebrated sea cotton dress

Her face was still caked

With a vision of grace

That used to make him squirm

While discovering what must be spent

To distinguish his desire from intent

And the lessons he did earn

Yet how many memories saved

In his lifelong hit parade

Could long stand abreast

With the hint of her caress

During the many games they played

And the promises that were made

In her celebrated sea cotton dress

Sagittarius A

Sagittarius A

Black hole center

Of the Milky Way

Absence of sound

So loud enshrouds

Dissonance of silence

Dissolving mong those a clouds

Hanging bal in the ance

In scattered dis

Array

Sagittarius A

Black hole center

Of the Milky Way

A clouds solve round

Mong clouds dis a day

Clouds solve mong a dis

Quilt crusty clay

With a pound

A steaming piss

And nothing much to say

 (Assuming the risk

Of course for flood

For delay and decay

For nuance and cud

For creating the obelisk

As well as the Scud

For engineering the

Improv

Ed and efficient Basilisk

And the hiss of raw lesions

In the quilt crack

Ed mud)

AfterKill

There is no announcement

Of pending doom

From the voice no longer lacing

The crowded room

With threads of word wool through

The waiting loom

Of sisters three and their mazy tomb

Of silence, of blindness and the boom

No voice remains

In that crowded room

No wool left over from

The weaver's loom

Constrained

By the loom lent from

The beaters flung

No longer can I maintain

The ballad for long

Or the control and the will

Over vocal strain

And bitter pill

Over local train

And window sill

Over counterpane

And free will

In a world insane

With afterkill

About the Author

Timothy Brannan is a Vietnam veteran (US Army Intelligence) poet, novelist, musician, composer, and painter born in Raleigh, North Carolina. He holds a Bachelor of Arts in English and Philosophy and a Master of Arts in Literature and Writing from NC State University. Both as an undergraduate and a graduate student he was mentored by the late Dr. Guy Owen (*Ballad of the Flim-Flam Man, Journey for Joedel, The White Stallion and Other Poems*). With Guy's encouragement, he submitted the first creative writing Master's thesis ever accepted at NC State University nearly thirty years before the university established an official MFA program. He also holds a Juris Doctor from Florida State University College of Law.

Contact the publisher or Timothy
info@geminipublish.com
www.geminipublish.com